Songs to Learn
& Sing
WHITE LABEL

Songs to Learn & Sing
20 Golden Greats

First published 2018 by The Hedgehog Poetry Press

Published in the UK by
The Hedgehog Poetry Press
Coppack House, 5
Churchill Avenue
Clevedon
BS21 6QW

www.hedgehogpress.co.uk

ISBN: 978-1-9996402-7-9

9 8 7 6 5 4 3 2 1

A CIP Catalogue record for this book is available from the British Library.

Songs to Learn & Sing

20 Golden Greats

by

Original Artists

SONGS TO LEARN & SING

With *Songs to Learn & Sing* we wanted to try something a little different. We challenged poets to choose their favourite song (or a favourite song, nobody has just one, after all) and from there they should shamelessly steal the title and then write a poem that responds to it. This response could be based on how the song makes them feel, a memory of where they heard it first or whatever it was that made it important in the first place.

This proved to be very popular and choosing Twenty from among them was all but impossible, but choose them you must and we were pleased to select Ceinwen Haydon's *I Want To Hold Your Hand* as the winner of our competition as it summed-up exactly what it was all about in the first place, although Ali Jones and Mick Yates, our Highly Commended Runners-Up, both could have taken the metaphorical Gold Disc on another day.

Songs to Learn & Sing is something a little different and we are sure that it will soon become a classic.

MD.

Side One

1. I WANT TO HOLD YOUR HAND
Ceinwen Haydon 9

2. BIRDMAD GIRL
Ali Jones 10

3. CASTLES MADE OF SAND
Mick Yates 11

4. AT LAST
Susan Castillo 12

5. I'M NOT IN LOVE
Kerry Darbishire 13

6. QUICKSAND
Steve Xerri 14

7. ALL THAT (BOTH SIDES NOW)
Mara Adamitz Scrupe 15

8. LETTER TO ME –
Gaynor Kane 16

9. RHAPSODY IN BLUE
Peter Francis Pegnall 18

10. FLIP, FLOP, FLY.
Zoë Sîobhan Howarth-Lowe 19

Side Two

1. GOD SAVE THE QUEEN
Chris Hemingway 20

2. RAGLAN ROAD
Marilyn Francis 21

3. WE ALL LIVE IN A YELLOW SUBMARINE
Betty Hasler 22

4. STATION TO STATION
Clare O'Brien 23

5. POKER FACE
Amy Alexander 24

6. ONE OF THESE NIGHTS
Mary Gilonne 25

7. I'M NOT IN LOVE
C.R. Smith 26

8. LA MER
David Mark Williams 27

9. WAY DOWN WE GO
Kerri Anne Stebbins 28

10. THE SOUND OF SILENCE
Dave Murray 29

I WANT TO HOLD YOUR HAND

for The Beatles

Ceinwen Haydon

even though mine's sticky,
smudged with ink. Under
my wooden desk, hidden,
I wriggle, press my thighs
together. Nice. Thoughts
I don't understand, but
I want to – will you?
You know, what I said?
Just fingers, entwined.

BIRDMAD GIRL
for The Cure

Ali Jones

What is it like? To wake in plumed morning,
sprouting feathered flames , blazing hot enough
to give the polar ice caps a run for their history.

An impossible dream of flight, lifting out
of night rooms, into other countries,
in a jangled tumble of words.

They say that you are mad, but maybe
you simply have another kind of wisdom,
found in the joy of thermals, the stab

of toothless sharp jaws, the ministry
of hard shelled eggs, the primitive soar and dip,
frenzied flocking, raved mobbing of roaring threats.

You open your throat to a bell of song,
a sky canvas dreamed in reverse, fantastical,
worlds beyond the veil of claw and tooth.

A northern child, thrown against the day's sighs,
to dive and breast away through open windows,
as light stepping through islands, going somewhere

in the sparring air, windward, your anchors lifted
and stowed behind your eyes, in secret places,
always ascending, flocking just out of reach.

CASTLES MADE OF SAND

for Jimi Hendrix

Mick Yates

did you ever

make sandcastles as a child

on the endless blue hot sunny days

in the long lost summers of childhood

when the tide was far out to sea?

digging deep channels for the moat

building high turrets from buckets

filled to the brim with still damp sand?

remember how impenetrable they seemed?

how firm and solid you constructed them?

then waiting for the tide to return

so confident in your building skills

so defiant in the strength of your architecture?

like the sandcastles you built way back then

nothing in this life is permanent

AT LAST

for Etta James

Susan Castillo

We drove down rose-flanked lanes
walked hand in hand
under the stars
drank champagne in Antibes.

We hailed taxis in Manhattan
You told me how you loved to say
'Fifth and Amsterdam!'
just like in the films.

We sailed down the Nile,
peeked into temples, tombs,
felt the presence of departed kings.
The thick dark made us shiver.

We basked on Caribbean sand
drinking cold beer in frosted bottles
from a beachfront shack,
Calypso tunes blaring on the radio.

In Paris, near the Musée Pompidou
We watched a man blow bubbles
shaped like fantastic beasts,
shimmering in the sun.

We found each other late in life
had such a short time to dance.
What a dance it was

I'M NOT IN LOVE

For 10CC

Kerry Darbishire

The names of the villages
belonging to that summer
escape me, but I remember
cramming the car with a tent,

sleeping bags, a dog, two children
the only cassette we could afford
and setting off for Wales.

Our first holiday, the song
that almost didn't happen,
rolled us along lanes, woods
by glimmering lakes, you smiling,

hand warm in mine mile after mile
past rivers smooth as the lyrics
and chords whispering hours to minutes

the sun tipping pine trees lipstick pink
until by starlight we could barely see
the road signs, unpronounceable
beginning and ending in 10cc.

QUICKSAND

For David Bowie

Steve Xerri

Shall I know you among the many who muster
beside me in colourless ranks in the holding bay?
Are there replacement names issued, should we

grab a face from the dressing-up box and stand
in line, re-enacting the jittery wait to step
from the wings to the stage? This time

we could be born beneath the same roof and live
quiet lives : or arrive in time of war, terrified
of gunfire wasting our young blood on the grass.

Shall I again see you from a seat in the gods
at the start of your career, meet you just the once
at an art show in your mint-green suit?

And will your new songs run a gold thread
through my days, so that I feel your next death
unravel something deep inside me, too? Or

are we so reshuffled that when you drop a coin
in my busker's cap you'll fail to recognise
the mismatched eyes that peer back out at you?

ALL THAT (BOTH SIDES NOW)
For Joni Mitchell

Mara Adamitz Scrupe

all that's severed & snapped & raggedy thrown down   now
       all that

all that's in & out tufts & wisps & never saw it coming numbed
         & scarred/ one root's sooty   one soft spot
one's missed the boat or blazing yellow

magic songbird fluted chill
            (another's furnace fever)   & me misty-eyed

all my loved & lost & lived *I know*   day in day out
        don't my voice grown thick
as smoke aside angels dreamt up late   *too late*

as prancing on a pinhead prick & semblance & false starts
        gelato on a stick   & how my many *many*

        & all that wake me up
suckler & despot & divine disorder *all that*

        all that's

        don't the spring scent of old roses & go-betweens
my good witch past selves' have me slid a little closer
        to the middle

        my annals & archives wised-up humbled still I shiver
& sway all that shimmy   & braggy full proud   once in a blue
        balancing the books

LETTER TO ME
For Brad Paisley

Gaynor Kane

Do not take advice from me.
You have foresight
and everything
happens for a reason.

Aren't you stronger
for knowing how close you came
to replicating the mistake
of your mother

but having the strength
to grab your bag and run
to the roundabout in bare feet
and nightie, never looking back?

Isn't your leg more interesting
for having the little dot-dot-dot, dash
dot-dot-dot faded stitch scar,
cut by a falling vase, as the phone cord

tried to strangle it,
when the Dubliner that you'd spent
a handful of hours face to face with
was proposing marriage?

Didn't you find out the fear
of being out of your depth
was irrelevant, when you were dragged
through the deep blue and survived?

How light you felt
moments before that, suspended
hundreds of metres above the coast of Zakynthos,
harnessed to your best friend?

Don't change
your wedding plans,
or doublecheck
that everything is packed.

RHAPSODY IN BLUE
For George Gershwin

Peter Francis Pegnall

if you were music I would switch you off,
you hypnotize me, you lull me like opium,
you net me like gossamer on gorse
you spider my soul into your private place
then you leave me to dry out and die.

I do not die, I join the circle
where lovers flap in the wind, chase their tails,
echo the same, dull song ad infinitum:
there they go again, getting older
 gracelessly, beaten before they start.

You are music and I adore you,
the more you play, the less I choose:
why should a fish fly? An orange blush?
You become the notes I don't recognize
in the wrong order. Bent, but not broken.

FLIP, FLOP, FLY.
For Ellis Hall

Zoë Siobhan Howarth-Lowe

Head-bob vibe music
mime to the man.
The muffled slang,
Hey guys, high-fives
jack-step, swish, jig jig;
yeah – fusion.
Ingenuity, throw in the moves,
high-kicks by the bagful
mock-spins and turns – go go go;
Jive baby.

GOD SAVE THE QUEEN
For The Sex Pistols

Chris Hemingway

The traditional English zeitgeist
was invented in 1977.
I woke up one morning
to the smell of hogs roasting,
and a tweed implosion
of morris bells and maypoles.

The traditional English zeitgeist
left me cold, but also fevered.
In my room, with the curtains drawn,
furiously turning the dial.
And it's 10cc, on the hour, but

not this one.
This black disc, blue sleeve,
is an institution too.
And if colour, sunshine, and melody
are pressed into national service,
then I'll take the grey,
the rain, this Detroit noise.
Under the skin, or torn into jackets.

And if the pins shine silver when they catch the light,
then it's my light,
my anthem.

RAGLAN ROAD

For Patrick Kavanagh

Marilyn Francis

It was early
and late, the glasses empty,
fire down to ash. You sang a poem,
a gift, you said, a present without strings.

When day came,
white and sharp as razors,
we walked to where the road began
and turned our separate ways.

But I still have the song
sometimes it catches me
when I'm walking somewhere
or looking out of the window
on rainy days.

It's like finding a pebble
in an old overcoat pocket
and it still tasting salt
and smelling of sea.

You sang me a poem.
A gift, you said.

WE ALL LIVE IN A YELLOW SUBMARINE
For The Beatles

Betty Hasler

They did live in a yellow submarine then,
and told each other fairy tales,
and waved from pink portholes
at those who did not live in the sun of their certainties;
not noticing that the sea was not really green
but shit brown, rank,
putrid with the stink of human nature
and clogged with the litter of intentions.

Of course the submarine sank.

Most of them survived,
struggling through tangled green weed
and crawling out
to find a wife and 2.2 kids
in a life of ordinary despair behind double glazing.

But some never made it:
and their bodies float face up
on the oceans of social history,
bloated and bruised blue,
their glazed white eyes wide
as if gazing through shattered glass
at a yellow submarine in the sun.

STATION TO STATION
For David Bowie 1947 – 2016

Clare O'Brien

The black star blossoms red, by gaslight and sodium
on wet tarmac. He beckons, but I am safe by my window.
The towers of asylum bloom dark as death
beyond the town, on a green hill far away.
                 I am driven in bright arterial flow
from the city to the sea. The red lights stalk me in my seat.
On school days I crossed the line by the bridge, down to the trolls
and the dead men in the morning.
          I stole, like you, while sweeter girls held roses.
I hoarded up my swag.   I did not see the electric fear,
the bloodflow north and south, hid what was burning bright
on either side of the Brighton line.
             Now, I have lost my bearings.
The lines have closed, the stations shifted.
In the dead days following your reversed resurrection,
I am carbonised in black, when red was what I wanted.

POKER FACE
For Lady Gaga

Amy Alexander

You and me in our meat dress
face the world, and it's less
blistering, less black and blue,
we're weird, and it's true--
it keeps the creeps away.
I never wanted to play
the sex doll, though you did,
sometimes, still, I noted,
it was never for the candy eyes,
from the makeup stool, you realized
you were hot sky
magic, this was all just dressing,
a hiding face, proud, no fessing
up, giant woman claiming her power
and poked fun at, still, not a care
in the world, Catholic girl, you go back
home and show up, your hair black
like it was when you were little
and they take you in, cattle
call school, Sister-What's-Her-Name
still loved you, there is no shame,
and that is mercy, the part of God
the men don't want to share, odd
girls together, bow our heads in prayer

ONE OF THESE NIGHTS .....

For The Eagles

Mary Gilonne

when heat bears down like a plummeting hawk,
and cows lounge in long heavy shadows. When
a gloam hangs on our hills as if grassed slopes
are glimmering slate and boundaries lost,
I'll leave you.

When from bed to wall lies a litter of windowed
 moons to use as stepping-stones, and light slices
through our kitchen thrum, as if your voice and mine
cut blunt with metallic glints of old licked knives.
I'll leave you.

When hands become so hollow that a wolf could hide
its prey, and uneasy trees shift with the bedded dark
of haunted things. When we disremember our earthy
days, and my garden lies scentless, empty as a cup.
I'll leave you.

One of these nights.....

I'M NOT IN LOVE
For 10CC

C.R. Smith

Staring meaningfully into space
fixating on photographs

screen-saved — wallpaper-displayed
surreptitiously taken. His messages

bombarding her mobile 24/7 — his poker face
denying midnight declarations.

This thing between them — something more?
These mixed messages confuse her.

What outcome does he internally debate?
Emoji daisies sent, received, erased.

Plucked petals
procrastinating fate ✿

LA MER

For Charles Trenet

David Mark Williams

An ear worm we can't stop,
soundtrack to our days,
along the Promenade Des Anglais,
film star police on horseback
poised to be snapped,
angels on roller blades brushing by,
their wings folded tight.
La Mer, the only words we know.
The rest we hum.
And our hearts go boum.
How well it fits that strip of blue
between the palm trees,
shading to jade at the littoral.
Across the carriageway
the sex workers cry,
flaunting sculpted bodies,
directing traffic.
Every evening the light softens,
dusted to gold, a large white bed.
La Mer becomes a black mirror
for whatever is bright,
gulls ghosting the dark sky.
A tea dance orchestra strikes up
in the ballroom of the bombed
and long gone pavilion,
a tune edged with the hiss of surf.
Clown-faced Trenet croons
into the Shure microphone
compelled to sing,
what else could he do?
La Mer, the only words we know.
The rest we hum.
And our hearts go boum.

WAY DOWN WE GO

For Kaleo

Kerri Anne Stebbins

[She learned to put on airs, to avoid stares
meant to catalogue and categorize her. She's more
resilient than she looks, but she's tired.
The truth makes you dig for it.]

She looks at strangers and friends staring
and dares them to do something:
Save her
Save themselves
Drown her in empathy
Show her how not to be
the girl returning to her seventh-grade classroom with death stuck in her hair. Show her

silver linings lodged in throats like the sediment that rushed into her father's lungs
before he had a chance to teach her how to lose him so young.

Show her how not to be the woman with her dad at the bottom of a river.

I don't pretend to be surprised when she dives into her madness and finds him there.
He's always been waiting, writhing, sinking
ahead of her,
his water-logged body rocking gently
in rhythm with waves that drowned him.

When I ask her why she says she's always been here:
This room with shattered glass
thrown across the bed like blankets.

THE SOUND OF SILENCE
For Simon & Garfunkel

Dave Murray

In the restaurant that ranks
number one in the online search
a couple are separated by a candle
that the waiter has only just lit
but neither says thank you.

Their downward faces are illuminated
by their screens, filter memories
of the places they've snapped
as they strolled through the city
their hands never made contact.

At times they forget where they are
they fill their mouths with slivers
of photos they feed to the world
a bicycle leant on a graffiti façade
a language they cannot translate.

They utter only in hashtags
to catch your fleeting attention
monochrome shadows in alleyways
a lone figure waiting on a platform
for the afternoon train home.

20 Golden Greats
Poetry For Pleasure

PFP